# Bake Infinite Pie with X+Y

Written By
**Eugenia Cheng**

Illustrated by
**Amber Ren**

L B

LITTLE, BROWN AND COMPANY
New York   Boston

To Liam and Jack,
from Aunt E

For my parents
—AR

## About This Book

The illustrations for this book were done in ink and Photoshop. This book was edited by Samantha Gentry and designed by Angelie Yap with art direction by Saho Fujii. The production was supervised by Kimberly Stella, and the production editor was Marisa Finkelstein. The text was set in Archer, and the display type is Mr Dodo.

**X and Y** are dreaming of pie.

X is imagining an infinitely wide pie
like an endless ocean or an open sky.

Y is longing for an infinitely tall pie
like a dizzying mountain or a tree growing high.

"How can we bake infinite pie when it isn't
real?" asks X, who is curious but cautious.

"We can find a way!" says Y, who is bold and
daring. "I know just who to ask."

Aunt Z can do anything with her brain.
She can create worlds large and small,
with giant beasts and tiny creatures.

When X and Y see the distant look
on her face, they know that means
she is thinking of a new dessert
or a four-dimensional dream.
X doesn't want to disturb her dream.
But Y is too excited. "Aunt Z!
Can you help us make infinite pie?"

Aunt Z thinks for a moment.

"There are infinite different ways to make pastry," she says. "We just need flour, butter, and water...but there are infinite possibilities for the amounts we use and ways we mix them."

"Let's start with an easy way," says X, who likes to take things nice and slow.
"Let's start with a hard way!" says Y, who sometimes goes unwisely fast.
Aunt Z smiles and starts getting ingredients out.
"First, we mix one part butter with two parts flour," she explains. "We rub it together with our fingertips, then mix in water and knead with our hands."

"What about with our elbows?" giggles X.

"What about with our feet?" jokes Y.

"Your fingers are more delicate," explains Aunt Z.

"And much cleaner!"

"Now let's roll out our pastry," says Aunt Z.
"I'll make a circle," says X, who likes building up to difficult things gradually.
"I'll make a triangle," says Y, who likes diving into difficult things straight away.
"I'll make a square," says Aunt Z.
The circle is the easiest to roll out!

"Now it's time to fill our pies!" says Aunt Z. "What filling shall we have?"
"I want banana because the slices are round like my pie," says X.
"I want strawberry because the slices are triangles like my pie," says Y.
"Are there any square-shaped fillings?" asks Aunt Z, gazing at her pie.
"Chocolate squares!" shout X and Y together.

"It seems to be taking infinitely long!" says Y.

"That's because you're excited," says Aunt Z. "It makes time seem infinite."

Finally, the pies are ready.

"It smells infinitely delicious," says X, who is easily pleased.

"But it's not really infinite, is it?" asks Y, who always wants more.

"Why don't you eat half?" says Aunt Z. "Now eat half of what you have left. Now eat half of what you have left again. You'll never finish, so your pie will last until infinity!"

"I like the corners the best," says Y.

"Aunt Z's square pie has the most corners," says X.

"What if we made a pie with 5 corners...6 corners...
7 corners...infinite corners...?" suggests Aunt Z.

"My round pie has infinite corners!" says X.

"But...it doesn't seem like it has *any* corners," says Y.

Aunt Z winks at them, knowing just what to do.

"Let's make infinite corners, pointy ones that you can really see!" says Aunt Z.

They roll out a very big circle, which Aunt Z cuts into a triangle.

"That only has 3 corners!"

says Y, who is not very patient.

"Aunt Z hasn't finished yet,"

says X, who is good at waiting.

Aunt Z begins to stick on some pieces of dough.

"It has 6 corners!" says Y.

"It has 12 if you count the ones pointing out
*and* pointing in," says X.

"Do those count as corners?" they ask.

"It's up to you," says Aunt Z, smiling.

"Now our star has even more corners!" says X.

"I've lost count!" says Y.

"It has 48," says X, who has been counting carefully.

Aunt Z sticks some more pieces on.

"Oh no, now I've lost count too!" says X.

"If we keep going forever, we'll have infinite corners...but properly pointy corners!" says Aunt Z.

"Let's not waste the leftover dough,"
says Aunt Z.
They roll it out into a big circle and
cut out 3 circles.
"No more circles will fit," says Y.
"Let's look for a smaller cutter," says Aunt Z,
rummaging around in a cupboard.
"I found one!" says X.

"*Now* no more circles will fit," says Y, who sometimes gives up too easily.

"Maybe Aunt Z has infinitely small cutters!" says X, who believes
in Aunt Z's powers.

"Close your eyes," says Aunt Z.

When they open them again she is holding a smaller cutter, and
a smaller one, and a smaller one....

"My pie goes on forever and ever!" says X.

"My pie goes all the way into the sky!" says Y.

"Are you happy with your infinite pie?" asks Aunt Z.

"Not yet!" shout X and Y.

"Let's make more difficult pastry," Y begs Aunt Z.

"We'll use more butter this time," says Aunt Z, mixing a little butter with the flour.

"That doesn't look like more," says Y doubtfully.

"Maybe we're not done yet," says X hopefully.

Aunt Z takes out a whole slab of butter
and wraps it in the dough like a package.
"Now fold it in 3 layers and roll it out again!"

"Now fold it in 3 and roll again!"
"3 times 3 is 9," says X thoughtfully.

"And again!" shouts Y. "That makes 27!"
"And again?" asks X. "That makes 81!"

"And again!" shouts Y again. "That makes 243!"
"And again?" asks X again. "That makes..."
"...729," says Aunt Z, pointing at her calculator.

"Are we making infinite layers?" asks X.

"We're making exponential layers," says Aunt Z. "The numbers grow fast with our folding! And we can watch the layers grow in the oven."

"It looks like it's growing to infinity!" says Y.

"Can you feel the layers melt on your tongue?"
asks Aunt Z. "The layers are almost infinitely thin."
"Making it infinitely delicious!" X and Y agree with delight.

"We'd better clean up," says Aunt Z. "But a clean kitchen just makes me want to bake more pie...."

"Let's bake more pie!" cheers X.

"And then every time we clean up, we'll bake some more pie!" says Y.

"We'll need an infinite kitchen to hold our infinite pie...," says Aunt Z.

"And infinite friends to share it with."

Dear Reader,

You might feel like you're afraid of math because you're not good at it, and you might feel like being afraid of math causes you to be no good at it. But I'd like to reassure you that it's okay to be afraid of it, because concepts like infinity can be daunting, just like there's something sensible about being afraid of heights. And in a way, that's the whole point: if we can get our heads around something daunting, then we've become more intelligent. Except unlike with heights, you can't really be injured doing math—you can always try again if you want to do it differently. The same goes for baking pie—just make sure you wear oven mitts when you take the hot pie out of the oven! I hope the concepts in this book make you think about math a little differently. Plus, everything is better when it's paired with pie!

Sincerely,
Dr. Eugenia Cheng

### IS INFINITY REAL?

X and Y begin the story dreaming of infinity, which mathematicians have done for thousands of years. Is infinity real? Is infinity a number? These are difficult questions to answer, and there isn't one right answer! It depends on what we mean by "real" and "number." There are many different kinds of numbers, and mathematicians through the ages have come up with more weird and wonderful ones.

### X- AND Y-AXES

X and Y represent children in the story, but in math they represent numbers when we don't know exactly what the numbers are, and they could be anything. When we draw graphs we often have a pair of straight lines as references, called the x-axis and the y-axis. The x-axis goes horizontally from side to side, and the y-axis goes vertically up and down. So X dreams of infinite pie stretching horizontally, whereas Y dreams of infinite pie stretching vertically.

### MATHEMATICAL WORLDS AND BEASTS

Aunt Z dreams of mathematical worlds and beasts all inside her head. Math can feel like we're counting and measuring things in the world around us, but it's really about *reasoning* with the world around us. Mathematicians don't just use measuring cups and spoons—they use imaginary tools that they dream up in their heads. Mathematical ideas can feel like a jungle, and we explore it by looking around to see what strange creatures we'll find lurking there. But this jungle and all the creatures are inside our imagination!

### INFINITE COMBINATIONS

Aunt Z starts with just three ingredients to make pastry: flour, butter, and water. But you can make infinite different types of pastry using different proportions and different methods for combining them. Pure math starts with a small number of basic ideas too, and there are infinite ways to combine them. Counting sounds like very basic math, but mathematicians count combinations of more complicated things, in a field called combinatorics.

## CROSS SECTIONS

When X and Y cut their fruit to make different shapes, those shapes are called cross sections. That's when you take a 3D shape, like a fruit, and cut it open to reveal a 2D shape across it. X cuts a banana to make circular cross sections, and Y cuts a strawberry to make triangular cross sections. You can make different cross sections depending on what direction you cut, and some fruits reveal beautiful mathematical patterns in their cross sections. Mathematicians study shapes and relationships between different shapes in geometry.

## ZENO'S PARADOX

Aunt Z suggests eating half the pie, and then half of what's left, and half of what's left again, and so on. This is a version of Zeno's paradox, named after the philosopher Zeno, who lived around two thousand years ago. A paradox is a situation that seems to defy logic in some weird and confusing way. Zeno was actually thinking about traveling from one place to another, not eating pie! Zeno's paradoxes eventually led to the mathematical field of calculus, which studies, among other things, how infinitely small things can be added up even though they're almost not there at all.

## POLYGONS AND CIRCLES

Y likes the corners of the pie, so Aunt Z makes pies with more sides to create more corners. A triangle has 3 sides, a square has 4, a pentagon has 5, and so on. If we keep making more sides, the shape becomes more like a circle. Does that mean a circle has infinite sides and infinite corners? Or does it have no sides and no corners? Or 1 side going all the way round? All these answers make sense, and there's no right answer! Shapes with straight edges are called polygons, and in the days before calculators and computers, mathematicians used them to make rough circles from straight lines, when curved lines were too difficult to understand.

## CONVEX AND CONCAVE

When Aunt Z makes a pie in the shape of a six-pointed star, Y thinks it has 6 corners, but X counts 12. That's because the star has 6 corners pointing out, but also 6 corners pointing in! X and Y wonder if those corners count. The answer is: it's up to you if you count them or not! Some shapes only have corners pointing out and none pointing in, and those shapes are called convex. The ones that have corners pointing in are called concave.

## FRACTALS

The star shape that Aunt Z makes is called the Koch snowflake. This is an example of a mathematical shape called a fractal. Fractals are amazing patterns with so much detail that if you keep zooming in on them, they look the same all the time. If you look at a small corner of the Koch snowflake and zoom in, it looks just like the Koch snowflake again. The shape Aunt Z makes with circles inside circles is another fractal called the Apollonian gasket.

## CONVERGING TO ZERO

When X and Y line their pies up in order of size, the pies get smaller and smaller, and if we kept going to an infinite number of pies it looks like they will disappear completely. In math this is called a convergent sequence. In this case the pies are becoming infinitely small and converging to zero! It's an important concept in calculus.

## EXPONENTIALS

X and Y make their puff pastry by folding it in 3 repeatedly. Each time they fold it in 3, they are multiplying the number of layers by 3. When we keep multiplying by the same number this is called an exponential. Exponentials start slow but then speed up and grow extremely fast. If we do it with the number 3 we get 3, 9, 27, 81, 243, 729, 2187, 6561...and after just 13 folds we'll be over a million!

## LOOPS

One way of creating infinity is by setting up a loop, where every time you get to the end of something it automatically starts again and will keep going forever! Aunt Z makes a loop in her kitchen because every time she bakes she cleans up afterward, but every time she has a clean kitchen she wants to bake more pie.

# BANANA BUTTERSCOTCH PIE

**FOR THE CRUST:**

1 cup all-purpose flour

½ stick of butter, cold and cut into small cubes

2–3 tbsp ice-cold water

**FOR THE FILLING:**

1 egg

¼ cup heavy cream

3 tbsp melted butter

¼ cup dark brown sugar (packed)

2 tsp all-purpose flour

pinch of salt (to taste)

2 medium bananas, sliced

1.  Pulse the flour and butter for the crust in a food processor (or rub between your fingertips) until it resembles bread crumbs.

2.  Stir in the water and then bring the dough together with your hands. Add more water, one teaspoon at a time, until the dough sticks together easily. Knead it lightly into a ball, wrap with plastic wrap, and chill in the fridge for 30 minutes.

3.  Roll out the crust and line your pie dish. Prick holes in the bottom with a fork. Bake at 400°F for 20–25 minutes until the crust is slightly browned. (If you want to be sure the crust won't puff up at this point, line it with foil and fill with baking beans or rice. Remove them for the last 5 minutes.)

4.  While the crust is baking, make the filling. Whisk the egg and the cream, then whisk in the melted butter, brown sugar, flour, and salt.

5.  When the crust is ready, arrange the banana slices in any pattern you like, and then pour the filling over it.

6.  Bake at 350°F for about 30 minutes until the filling is golden and bubbly. Serve warm with ice cream or chilled topped with whipped cream!